PATTERN TRADING FOR BEGINNERS

Tools and Strategies in 90 minutes

Daeshim Park

Table of the Contents:

Chapter I

Monkey business

Once upon a time, a wealthy businessman arrived
in a small village.He told the people that he would
buy monkeys for $100 each.
After all, there were hundreds of monkeys in a neighboring
forest, so theresidents were thrilled.

They captured the monkeys and delivered them to the
businessman.

He purchased hundreds of monkeys and paid the villagers
$100 for each one theygave him.

The villagers started getting monkeys from the forest and
selling them to thebusiness man to make a living.

Soon, the forest began to run out of easy-to-catch monkeys.

The businessman, sensing this, makes an offer of $200
for each monkey.The villagers were delighted.

They returned to the forest, set up traps, captured the monkeys, and gave them tothe businessman.

After a few days, the wealthy man declared he would pay $300 per monkey.

The villagers started climbing trees and risking their lives to capture monkeysand deliver them to the businessman who had purchased them.

In the forest, there were no more monkeys!

The businessman said one day that he wanted to acquire additional monkeys for $800 each.

The people couldn't believe what they were hearing. They were eagerlyattempting to acquire more monkeys.

Meanwhile, the wealthy man informed that he needed to return to the city forsome business and that his manager would handle it on his behalf until he returned.

The villagers were disappointed once he went.

They could make quick money by selling monkeys, but the forest was empty ofmonkeys.

This was when the wealthy man's manager intervened.

He gave the villagers an offer they couldn't refuse.
He showed the villagers all the monkeys that the
wealthy man had caged.He assured the residents that
he would sell the monkeys for $400 each.
"When the rich man returns, sell them to him for 800$
each," the manager said.The residents were again thrilled.
They calculated the math. You can buy it for $400 and
sell it for $800.They'd just discovered the most
efficient way to double their money.
The people gathered all of their funds and even took out a
loan.

There were enormous lines, and the manager sold out
practically all of themonkeys within a few hours.

Unfortunately, their joy was short-lived since the manager
vanished the next day,and the wealthy man never returned.

Many villagers kept the monkeys, hoping the wealthy man
would return.

However, they quickly lost hope and released the monkeys
back into the forestbecause feeding and caring for the noisy
monkeys had become very difficult.

This story is the perfect way to explain how the Financial markets work.

The wealthy businessman represents the key players in the capital markets like corporate Financial institutions, investment banks, and foreign institutional investors. On the other hand, the villagers represent the new and ordinary traders trading in the market.

The key players fool the ordinary traders by manipulating the stock price movements in a short time by buying in or selling in bulk quantities.

Seeing this, ordinary traders misunderstand it as an opportunity to make profitsand enter trades by buying or selling financial assets.

Once they all are in, these smart traders go in the opposite direction, taking away all the capital money of ordinary traders.

Once the ordinary traders realize it, it will be too late. So they end up losing all their money.

So, is there any way to stop this from happening?

The quick answer is to do a thorough analysis before entering every trade. This is where technical analysis helps.

Let's call it Plan A.

By this, It is possible to formulate a logical certainty regarding the price movement, and understand the safe entry and exit points of every trade, thereby protecting the trading capital.

But what if the technical analysis fails?

Even if technical analysis fails, investors can still protect their trading capital.Let's call it Plan B, which is Trade discipline.
The upcoming chapters will examine and explain these concepts.

It is said that about 90% of people doing intraday trading end up in losses.4% neither make a loss nor any profit.
Only 6% of traders become successful.

They are known as professional or intelligent traders.
Why do 90% of people trading in the stock market fails?

They fail because:

1) They don't research the stock, currency, or commodity they are trading.

2) They trade without having any plan or trading strategy.

3) They follow too much on other people's recommendations.

4) They don't have any trade discipline.

Remember, in financial markets, the loss of one person is another person's profit. There is a 90 - 90 - 90 Rule in the Stock market industry.

The rule states that:
"90% of traders lose 90% of their capital within the first 90 days of accountopening!"

The 6% smart and intelligent traders enjoy the loss made by 90% of total traders. Please note that the 6% traders become large numbers when considering the total number of traders.

Many people enter into trades just because everyone else around them is doing it, and they most probably end up in losses. If you need to become one of the most successful traders in the stock market, you need to do the opposite of what the other 90% of ordinary traders do.

Yes, you heard it right.

Swim against the current, which is the ultimate secret for successful trading. That is the purpose of this book.

"To enable all traders to make consistent, profitable trades with ease and grace to achieve financial freedom."

Technical Analysis

Technical analysis examines price trends and chart patterns to evaluate investments and identify trading opportunities. In technical analysis, past tradingactivity and price changes can be good indicators of what the security's price will doin the future.

Trend : In technical analysis, a trend is a sustainable direction of price movement. Trends describe the general direction of a market or an asset's price. Letus learn a few basic terminologies for better understanding:

Trend line : A straight line drawn on a chart connecting the price's highs or lows shows the price movement's general direction.

Higher high : When a price makes a new high crossing above the previous high level, such a development (surge) is often defined as a Higher High price movement.

Higher low : When a price makes a new low more elevated than the previouslow, it is termed a Higher low.

Lower High : When a price goes down and makes a new

High below the previous High level, it is called a Lower High.

Lower low : When a price goes down and makes a new low below the previous low, the trend is described as a Lower Low.

Breakout : In technical analysis, a breakout occurs when the price moves abovea resistance level or downwards below a support level. A breakout indicates a potential trend in the breakout direction.

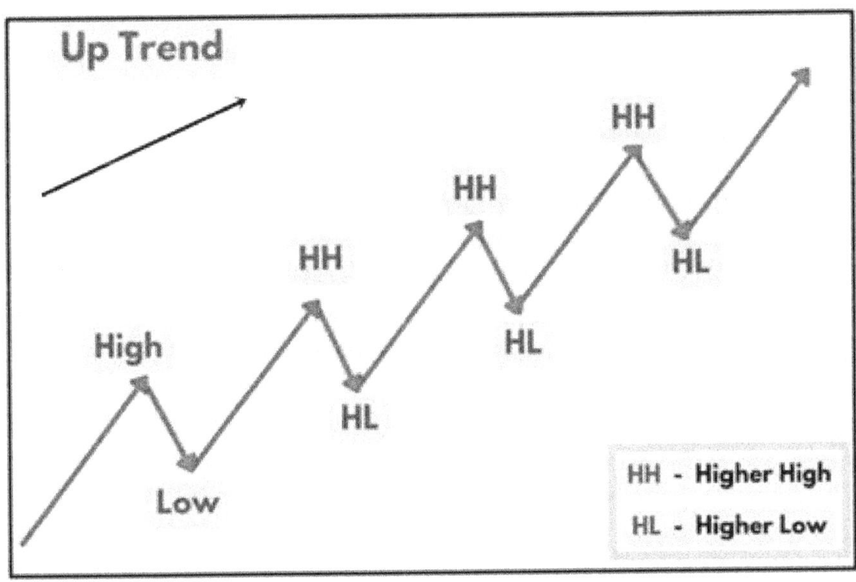

An uptrend is the price movement of a financial asset when the overall directionis upward. That means it goes up and down practically with higher highs and higher lows over some time.

Looking up the chart, the continuous movement of prices scales new highs, breaking the previous highs. This is the essential requirement for BUYING a Stockor commodity. A stock can trend upwards, downwards, or sideways for extended periods (days, weeks, or months).

How long does it take for a stock to qualify as in an uptrend?

Technically speaking, as soon as you see three consecutively higher high prices with higher lows in between those highs, you can say that you have set up anupward-trending price pattern.

The above chart shows the price chart of Crude oil futures. The price is movingin the upward direction making new highs. The price took a U-turn from the downtrend to uptrend from point A (Low) to Point B(High).

The price moved upwards, creating new Higher highs (HH) and recent Higher Lows (HL).

The uptrend is confirmed when the price made three consecutive Higher highsand three higher lows.

This uptrend will change direction to a downtrend on forming three consecutive Lower highs and lower lows.

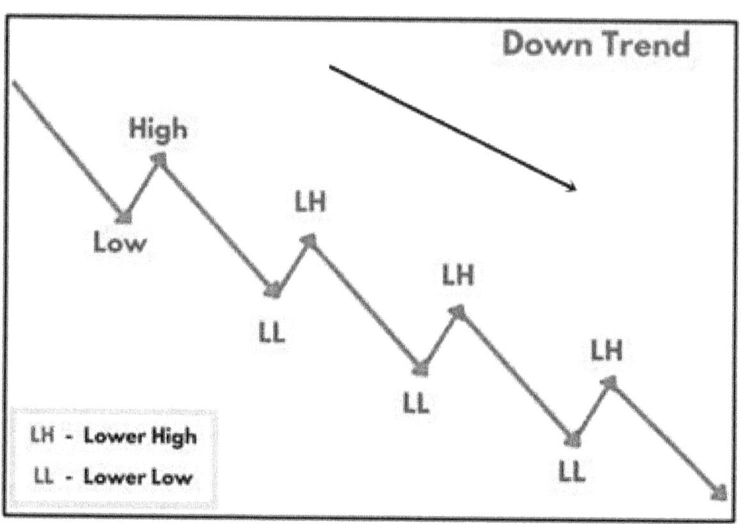

Downtrend: This is just the opposite of an Uptrend. Here the overall direction is downward. The price moves downward continuously with lower highs and lowerlows. A downward trend is identified when there are three consecutive lower lows with lower highs between those lows, which means the SELL Mode is ON.

Rule of thumb: Most of the time, price breakouts happen in the trend direction.

The above chart shows the price chart of Gold/USD. The price is moving in thedownward direction making new lower lows.

From point B onwards, the price direction changed from an uptrend to adowntrend.

The price moved downwards, creating new Lower highs (LH) and Lower Lows(LL).

The downtrend is confirmed when the price made three Lower Lows and threelower Highs.

This downtrend will change direction to an uptrend on forming three consecutiveHigher Lows and Higher Highs.

Trend Line

A trend line is a straight line drawn on a chart connecting the highs or lows of the price, which shows the general direction of the price movement. The trendline acts as a diagonal support or resistance. A trendline is formed by connecting the first and second lows or highs. The price usually breaks out of a trend line on the fourthor fifth touch.

The above figure shows EURO/USD 1-hour price chart. Here the trend line is formed by connecting the first and second lows. The third and fourth touch validates the trend line, and the price breaks out of the trend line on the fifth touch.

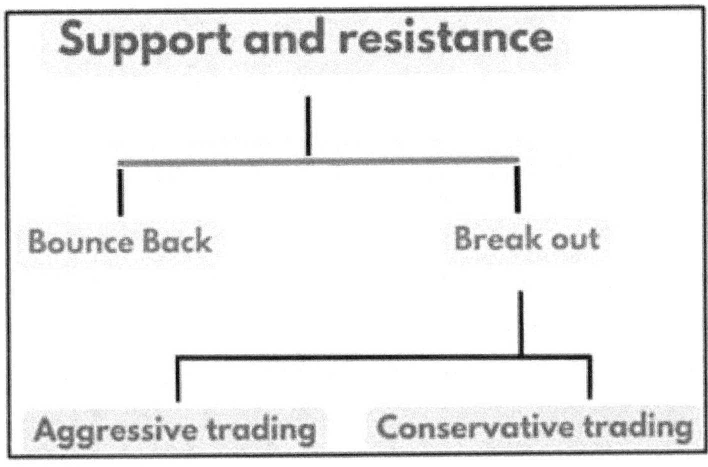

The price movement of an asset usually happens between a support and a resistance. The price hit the support and resistance line repeatedly and bounced back between the levels. After bouncing back for some time, the price Breaks out either from the support or the resistance level, which creates an opportunity to enter atrade. There are two ways to enter a trade when a breakout happens.

1. **Aggressive trading.**
2. **Conservative trading.**

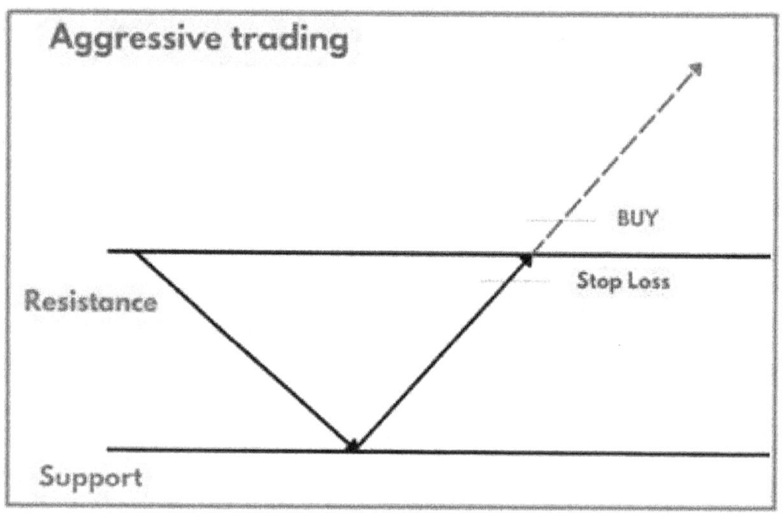

Aggressive trading is a strategy used by retail traders and individual investors to generate quick returns. Aggressive trading refers to quickly opening and closingpositions, with rapid entry and exit in different market scenarios. Typically, traders hold their positions for only a few hours or days before exiting the positions tocapture small gains (and avoid losses).

Advantages: Bigger profits: If the trading decision is correct, it can result in more significant gains because of a sudden price change.

Disadvantages: This trading method is a bit risky because of the quick BUY and SELL happening at critical points of price movement. If the decision is wrong, itcan make huge losses.

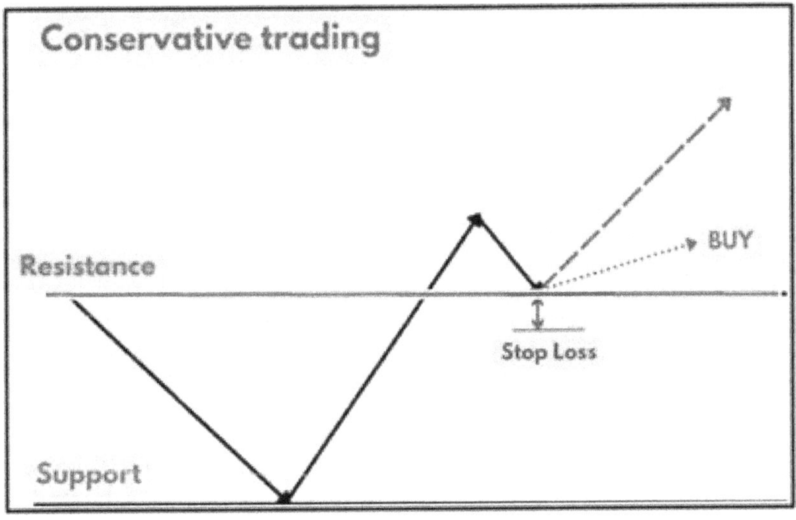

The goal of conservative trading is to preserve the purchasing power of one's capital with the least amount of risk. Therefore, traders who use conventional trading strategies combine fundamental and technical analysis to make well-informed decisions about trade. When there is a price breakout, they wait for confirmation to enter the trades.

Therefore, they tend to trade over more extended periods since doing that much analysis is time-consuming. Conservative trading requires patience and discipline.

Advantages: Less risky, High success rate, More chance of ending up in profit than aggressive trading

Disadvantages: This method is time-consuming. Less profitable than aggressive trading.

Chapter II
Pattern Trading

Most Analyzed and Highly Effective Patterns

Pattern trading is an integral part of Technical analysis. Successful and professional traders widely use it to trade stocks, currencies, and commodities.

Over time, patterns are formed by lines connecting price points, such as closing prices or highs and lows.

Price patterns often indicate a change between rising and falling trends.

In every price chart, the price's continuous movement results in specific shapes identified using a set of trendlines and curves.

Each price pattern has a unique set of characteristics. By understanding these unique characteristics, one can predict in which direction the price will probablymove when a price pattern formation is completed in a chart.

A price chart may consist of many different price patterns. However, specific patterns are often discussed and analyzed by experienced traders worldwide. Theseare called 'Signal' Patterns or 'Signs.'

The following are the sixteen most analyzed and highly effective patterns topredict the price movement of financial instruments. We will discuss different patterns in detail regarding their characteristics, interpretation, and how to use them effectively in real-time trades.

The Double Top Pattern

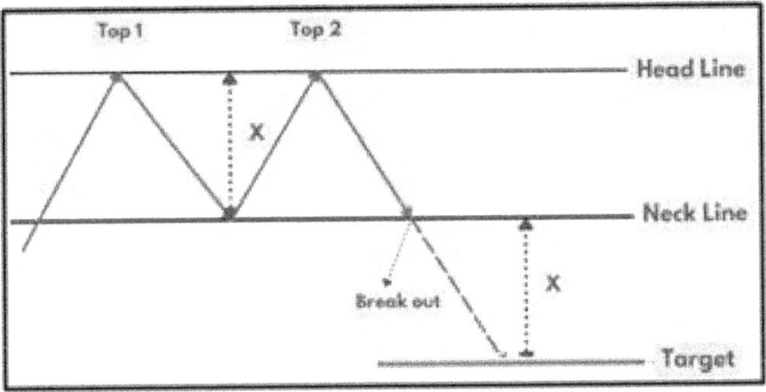

Figure 1.1

In technical analysis, a double top pattern is a reversal chart pattern when prices make two successive peaks at approximately the same price level(Resistance) butfail to continue rising beyond that level-

This pattern has the shape of the Letter "M." The top part of "M" acts as the resistance level and the bottom as support.

The resistance level is too strong, which won't easily allow the price to break thatlevel and go upwards. It is a very reliable indication of bearish sentiment in anasset. This pattern indicates that upward momentum has stalled before achievingnew highs. As such, it is considered a bearish continuation pattern. The price goes down towards the support, and once it breaks the support(It happens in most cases),it will go further down.

Rule of thumb:

When a double top is formed, do the following:

1. Draw a horizontal line connecting the Top/Heads of the first and second peaks(The top part of the "M" shape). It is called the Headline.

2. Draw a horizontal line that passes through the base level from where the peaksstarted

(The bottom part of the "M" shape). It is called the Neckline.

3. The distance (X) between the Headline and Neck Line is the new targetdownwards, starting from the Neckline (The total height of the "M" shape).

4. Thumb rule: Make sure the tops of two peaks are almost on the same level. The maximum variation for an ideal Double top is between 1% to 0.5% of the price.

Example: Price of Stock 1000 RS.

Case 1: First peak 1000 and second peak 1005. It is a Valid Double Top

Case 2: First peak 1000 and second peak 1030. It is NOT A Valid Double top

Tip: Traders can use indicators (mentioned in chapter IV) to confirm beforeentering any position.

Figure 1.2

Figure 1.2 shows the weekly(Long term trade) price chart of AUD/USD.

Here the price rose, hitting the resistance line and falling back to the nearest support level, forming the first peak(Top1). The price then bounced back upwards,hit the resistance line again, and fell back to the same level, forming the second peak (Top 2).

This completes the Double top pattern setup. The

horizontal line crossing through the bounce-back level is the Neckline. The price difference between the Neckline and the resistance Line connecting the two tops (X) is the target for the following support.

The Double Bottom Pattern

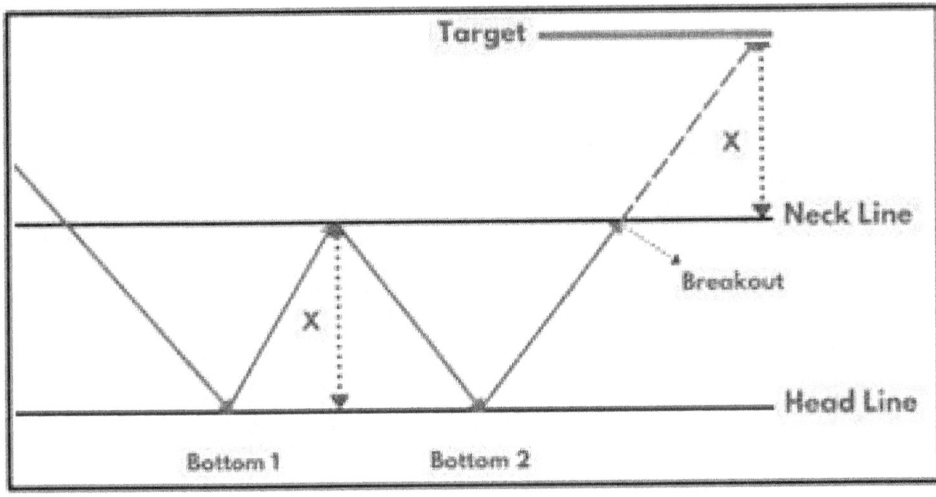

Figure 2.1

A double bottom pattern is a reversal pattern found at either end of a trend.This pattern has the shape of the Letter "W."

As the name suggests, the Double bottom pattern has Two bottom points atalmost the same level.

The horizontal line connecting the two bottoms becomes a strong support level which will cause the falling price to bounce back upwards.

Usually, this bounce back causes upward solid movement towards the resistance level(The top section of "W"), A break above this price point confirms that upward trend and completes the pattern.

Professional traders trade Double top/double bottom patterns only if there is aclear indication of strength after confirmation, as a false signal can result in losses.

Rule of thumb:

When a double bottom is formed, Do the following:

1. Draw a horizontal line connecting the bottom points (inverted peaks) of the first trough and the second trough(Bottom part of "W" shape - Headline).

2. Draw a horizontal line that passes through the top level from where the troughs started (Top part of "W" shape - Neckline).

3. The distance (X) between the Headline and Neck Line is the new target upwards, starting from the Neckline. (The total height of the "W" shape)

4. Make sure the bottom points of the two peaks are almost on the same level. The maximum variation for an ideal Double bottom is between 1% and 0.5% of the price.

Figure 2.2

Figure 2.2 shows the daily price chart of the US Dollar/Japanese Yen.

Here the price movement resulted in the formation of two troughs (Bottom 1 &Bottom 2) almost at the same level.

The Neckline is X points away from the support line connecting the two bottompoints.

The target is X points from the Neckline in the upward direction.

The Rectangular Pattern

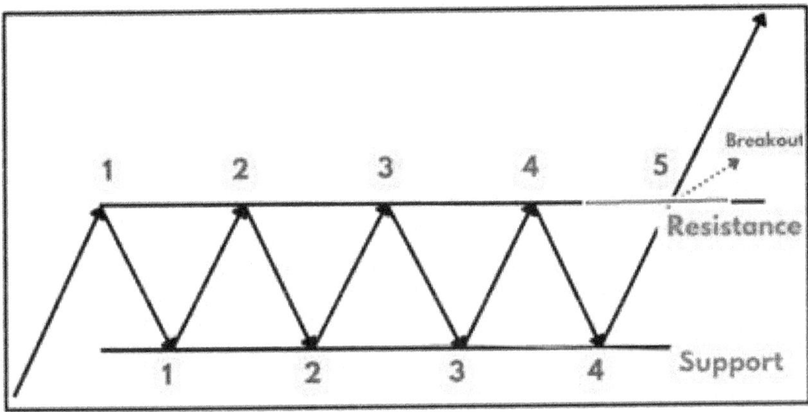

Figure 3.1

A rectangular channel or Box channel pattern is formed when the price of anasset moves in between two horizontal trendlines parallel to each other.

The price moves between horizontal support and resistance for some time,indicating a period of consolidation or indecision between buyers and sellers.

The price will touch the support and resistance line for some time before itbreaks out of the channel pattern.

The direction of the trend determines which direction the rectangular pattern willbreak out.

Rule of thumb:

1. A channel is formed by three consecutive peaks/troughs.

2. All points must touch the channel trendlines at the top/bottom for every bounce back.

3. In an uptrend, the Rectangular channel usually breaks at the resistance line.

4. In a downtrend, the Rectangular channel usually breaks at the support line.

5. The price usually breaks out on the fourth or fifth touch on the support or resistance line.

6. When the price breaks out of the channel, the first target is the width of the channel. (If the channel width is 'X'

points, then the price will break up or down 'X' points).

7. When a rectangular channel is formed, most traders prefer to wait for the breakout to enter the trades.

8. Aggressive traders prefer to trade the channels by buying near the bottom and selling or shorting near the top of the channel to take advantage of the price bouncing.

Figure 3.2

Figure 3.2 shows the daily price chart of Micron Technology Inc.

The price moved horizontally by bouncing between

points 1 and 4 for some time, forming a rectangular channel pattern. Here there is indecision between buyers and sellers. Then the buyers became intense, and the price suddenly moved upward, breaking out from point 4, resulting in a sharp price increase.

The price moved X points upward to the first target, which is the height of the rectangular channel.

Ascending Channel Pattern

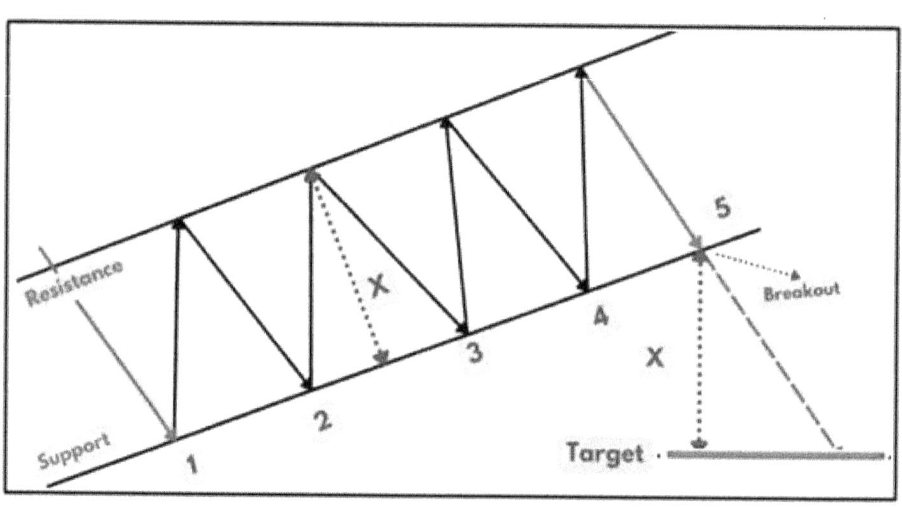

Figure 4.1

An ascending channel is the price action movement between two upward-sloping parallel lines. This pattern often appears in a downtrend.

The line on top connects the higher high, and the bottom line connects the lower lows of the asset price. The price inside the channel usually bounces between its support and resistance lines until it breaks out of the channel.

Aggressive traders use the channel patterns to enter and exit trades whenever the price touches the channel lines.

The channel patterns help the traders to get some clarity about the future price movement.

For example, Aggressive traders usually go for a Buy when the channel touchesthe support, expecting the price to bounce from the bottom support line.

In the same way, they go for a Sell when the price touches the top resistancelevel of the channel.

The conservative traders wait for the channel to break to enter the trade to benefitfrom the expected significant price movement.

Rule of thumb:

1. The price movement inside an Ascending channel usually breaks at the support line.

2. The price breaks downwards from an Ascending channel onthe 4th or 5th touch on the support line.

3. When the price breaks downside, the first target is the width of the channel. (If the width of the channel is 'X' points, then the price will break downwards 'X'points)

Figure 4.2

Figure 4.2 shows the forex daily price chart of NZD/USD.

Here the price bounced between the two rising parallel lines, forming anascending channel.

The price broke out of the ascending channel on the fourth touch on the supportline.

The price came down X points(the width of the channel) to reach the next target.

Descending Channel Pattern

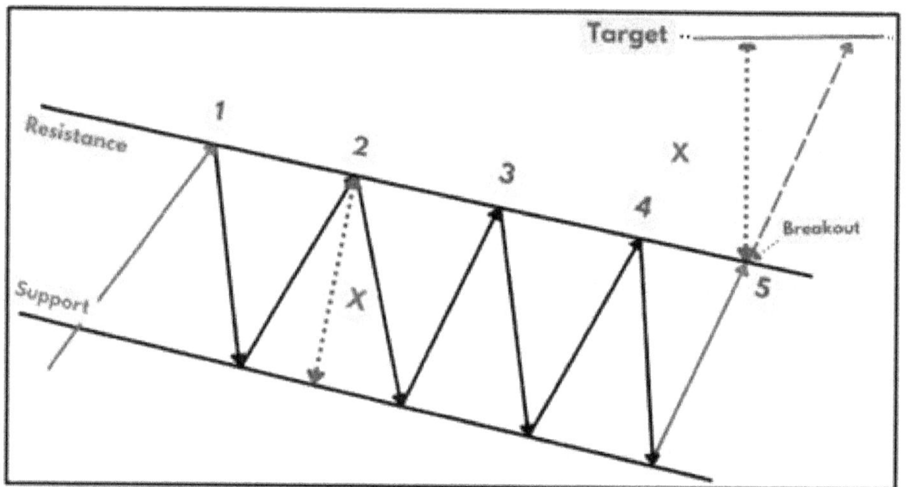

Figure 5.1

Descending channel is just the opposite of Ascending channel. It is formed by connecting lower highs and lower lows of the price of a security with two parallel lines. A descending channel shows a downward trend just before an upward price movement. A descending channel often appears in an uptrend.

Even though the descending pattern indicates possible bullish movement, traders usually use this pattern to buy and sell whenever the price touches the upper orlower channel line, carefully watching for a breakout. The price movement will be much faster when the price breakout happens than inside the channel.

Rule of thumb:

1. The price movement inside a Descending channel usually breaks at the Top side.

2. The price breaks out upwards from a descending channel onthe 4th or 5th touch on the Resistance linc.

3. When the price breaks upwards, the first target is the width of the channel. (Ifthe width of the channel is 'X' points, then the price will break upward 'X' points)

Figure 5.2

Figure 5.2 shows the Forex daily price chart of NZD/JPY.

The figure shows a reversal of the trend direction.

The price fell to bounce from the support line to point one, and then it bouncedbetween two falling parallel lines, forming a descending channel pattern.

Here the sellers tried to lower the asset's price, but in the end, the buyers won.

The price broke out of the Descending channel X points upward from point 5 toreach the next target.

Bullish Flag Pattern

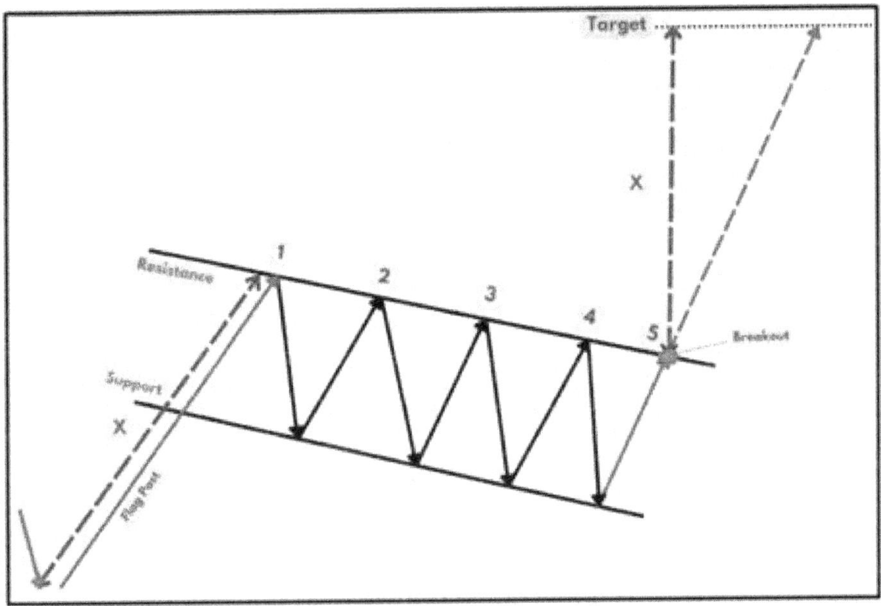

Figure 6.1

The Flag pattern is a continuation pattern. As the name suggests, the flag pattern looks like a flag. It is very similar to Channel Patterns with an attached Flag pole.

A bullish flag shows a sharp increase in the asset's price. Then it will start tomove sideways between a support and resistance level parallel to each other. The result is a descending channel and indecision area for buyers and sellers.

Usually, in a bullish flag, the price breaks the resistance level and continues to move upward. Once the breakout happens, there will be a sharp increase in theasset's price. The length of the flag pole is considered its target in the upward direction.

Rule of thumb:

1. The Flag pattern is a continuation pattern.

2. The price movement inside a Bullish Flag Pattern usually breaks at the Topside.

3. The price breaks out upwards from a Bullish flag on

the 4th or 5th touch onthe Resistance line.

4. When the price breaks upwards, the next target is the height of the Flag post/pole. (If the size of the flag post is 'X' points, then the price will break upward'X' points)

5.

Figure 6.2

Figure 6.2 shows the Forex 30 minutes price chart of the US Dollar/Swiss Franc.Here there was a sharp increase in price, forming the flag pole(X points)

Then the price consolidated in between a Descending channel pattern, indicatingindecision between buyers and sellers.

Then the buyers became stronger again, and the price moved upward to the targetX points from the break-out point.

Bearish Flag Pattern

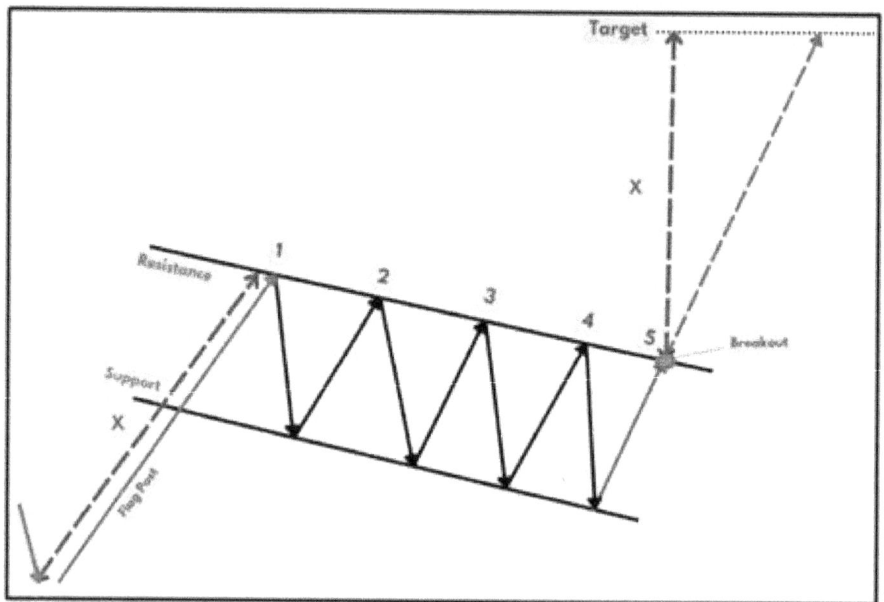

Figure 7.1

A Bearish Flag pattern indicates possible future price movement in thedownward direction. It is just the opposite of the Bullish flag pattern.

The steady price movement in the downtrend forms an ascending channel. The price then bounces between the channel support and resistance line before breakingout of the channel. Once the breakout happens in a bearish flag pattern, the price movement in the downward direction will be much faster.

Rule of thumb:

1. The price movement inside a Bearish Flag Pattern usually breaks at thedownside.

2. Most of the time, the price breaks out downwards from a Bearish flag onthe 4th or 5th touch on the Support line.

3. When the price breaks downwards, the next target is the height of the Flag post/pole. (If the size of the flag post is 'X' points, then the price will break downwards 'X' points)

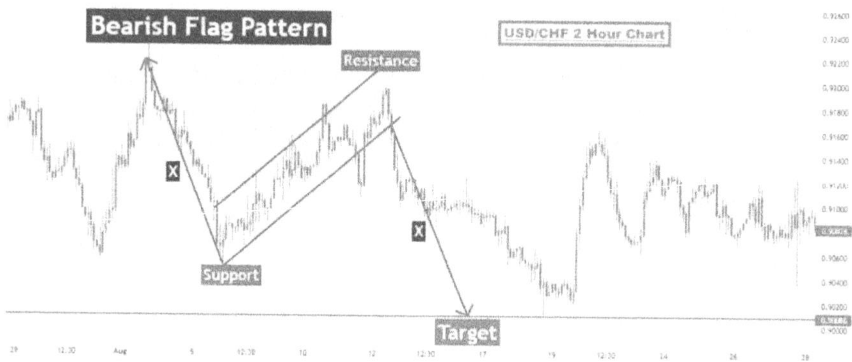

Figure 7.2

Figure 7.2 shows the Two-hour Forex price chart of the US Dollar/ Swiss Franc.

Here the price moved almost like a Double bottom. However, the pattern failedto complete the Double bottom since the price took a U-turn before reaching the Neckline.

The price moved in the form of an inverted flag, resulting in the price breakingout of the flag pattern downwards.

The price moved X points (the length of the flag post) down to hit the targetlevel.

Ascending Triangle Pattern

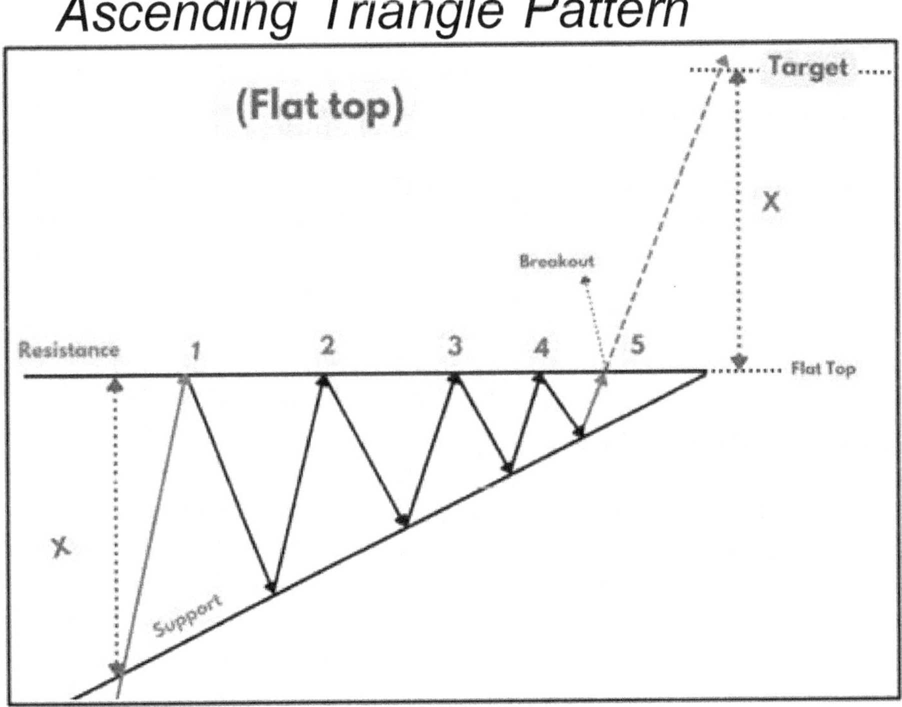

Figure 8.1

An ascending triangle is also known as a rising triangle. It is one of the top continuation patterns which appears in the middle of a trend. It is formed by ahorizontal trendline connecting swing highs and a rising trendline connecting the swing lows. These two lines form a triangle. Ascending Triangle indicates the possible continuation of price in the upward direction. The resistance line is almostflat and remains unchanged, while the support line rises with price movement. The rising trendline shows that the buyers are more substantial than the sellers. When the price breaks upwards, the pattern is completed.

Rule of thumb:

1. The price movement inside an Ascending triangle usually breaks at theTopside.

2. Most of the time, the price breaks out upwards from Ascending Triangle on

the 4th or 5th touch on the Resistance line.

3. When the price breaks upward, the next target is the height of the Triangle. (Ifthe height of the Triangle is 'X' points, then the price will break upward 'X' points)

4. The Ascending Triangle is considered valid when formed in an uptrend.

Advantages: This pattern is easy to identify and has target-level clarity.

Figure 8.2

Figure 8.2 shows the daily price chart of the stock Walgreen boot.

The price movement could not break the first resistance line(Marked as support). The price failed to break the resistance lines many times, but it started to consolidate closer to the resistance line.

Here the price is making newer Higher lows, with the top-level remaining thesame by creating Ascending channel pattern. The price broke out of the resistanceline on the fifth touch and moved upwards. The price hits the target **X** points up, which is the height of the Ascending triangle.

Descending Triangle Pattern

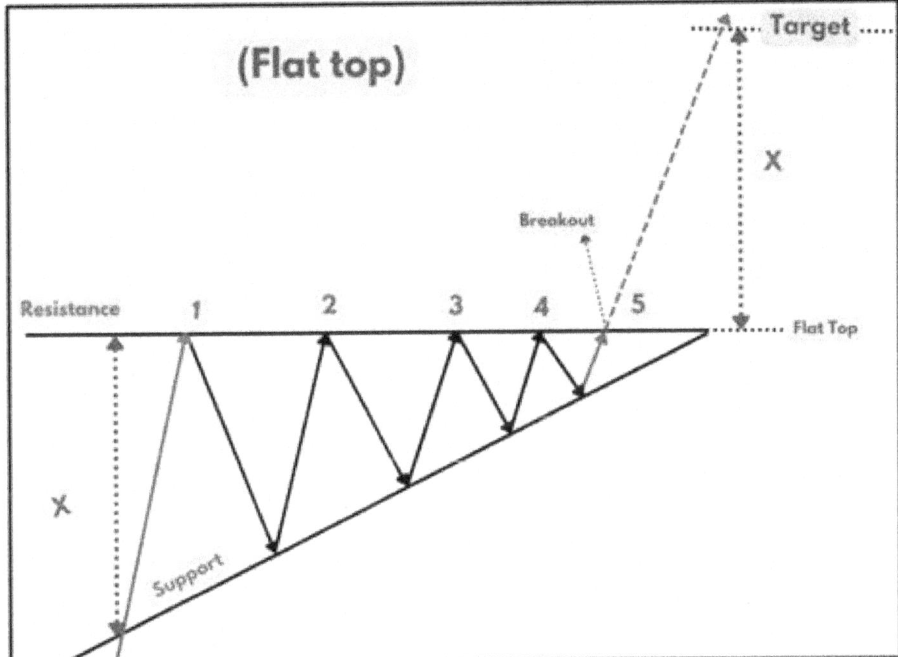

Figure 9.1

A Descending triangle, or the falling triangle, is a bearish continuation pattern.This pattern shows that sellers are more vital than buyers. A descending triangle consists of a horizontal trend line connecting the lows and a falling trend line that connects the highs. The support line is almost flat, and the resistance line is descending downwards. The breakout happens downwards from the support line. When the price starts to form a descending triangle pattern, traders usually order to open a short position(SELL) at the support level with a stop loss placed above the resistance level.

Rule of thumb:

1. The price movement inside a Descending triangle Pattern usually breaks at thedownside.

2. The price breaks downwards from a Descending triangle on the 4th or 5th touch on the Support line.

3. When the price breaks downwards, the next target is the height of the Descending triangle. (If the height of the triangle is 'X' points, then the price will break downwards 'X' points)

4. The Descending Triangle is considered valid when formed in a downtrend.

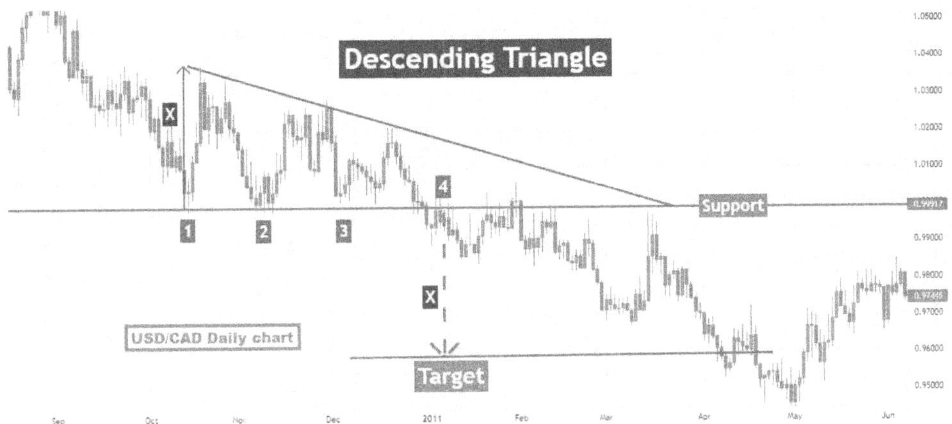

Figure 9.2

Figure 9.2 shows the forex daily price chart of the USD/CAD.

Here, the price movement could not break the first support line.The price failedto break the support level many times, but it started to consolidate closer to the support. From the chart, it is evident that the price is making newer Lower highs, with the bottom level remaining the same by creating a Descending channel pattern. The price broke out of the support line on the fourth touch and moved downwards.

The price hit the target X points down, which is the height of the Descending triangle.

Symmetric Triangle Pattern

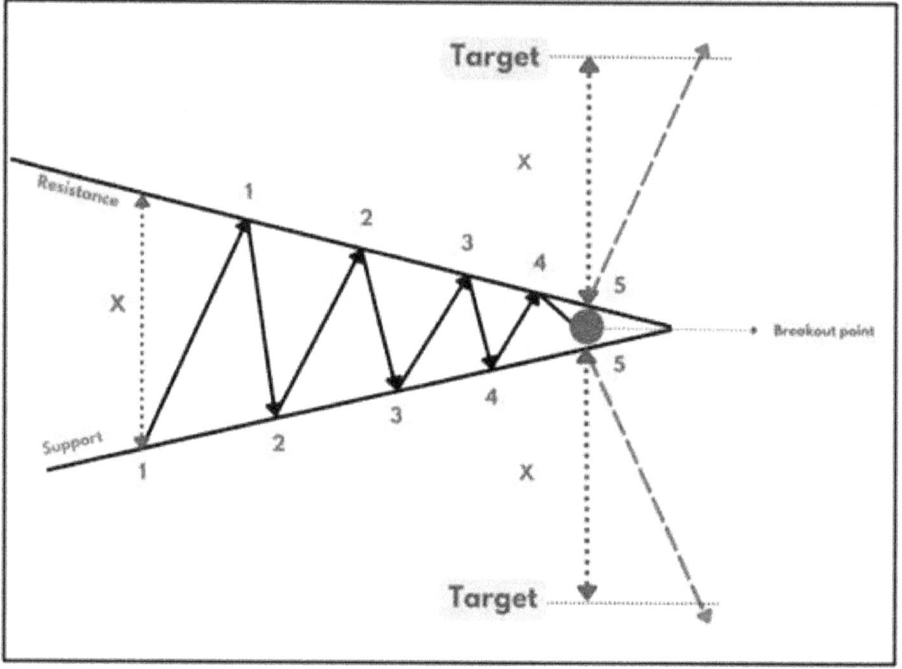

Figure 10.1

A symmetric triangle is a combination of Ascending triangles and descending triangles. Symmetric triangles are neutral patterns, which means the breakout can occur either upwards or downwards. It is impossible to predict in which directionthe breakout will happen. Most smart traders expect a symmetric triangle to breakout in the direction of the trend. Traders often watch for breakouts from a symmetric triangle to enter trades in the price movement direction. If in an uptrend, a possible breakout of the symmetrical triangle would be in the upward trend and vice versa. Following a breakout from a symmetric triangle, traders tend to buy or sell aggressively, according to the price's direction.

Rule of thumb:

1. The price movement inside a Symmetrical triangle Pattern could break out upward or downward.

2. The price breaks out and often happens on the 4th or 5th touch on the Supportor Resistance line.

3. When the price breaks downwards or upwards, the next target is the height ofthe Symmetric triangle. (If the height of the triangle is 'X' points, then the price will break downwards or upwards 'X' points)

4. In many cases, a symmetric triangle breakout happens in the direction of the trend.

Figure 10.2

Figure 10.2 shows the Gold spot/US Dollar Daily price chart.

Here the price made a new High, then a few consecutive higher lows (HL), then lower Highs (LH) almost three times. This price consolidation resulted in the formation of a Symmetric Triangle.

In the above chart, the buyers became more potent than the sellers, and the price broke out of the Symmetric triangle in the upward direction.

The target is the height of the symmetric triangle(X

points) in the upward direction.

Rising Wedge Pattern

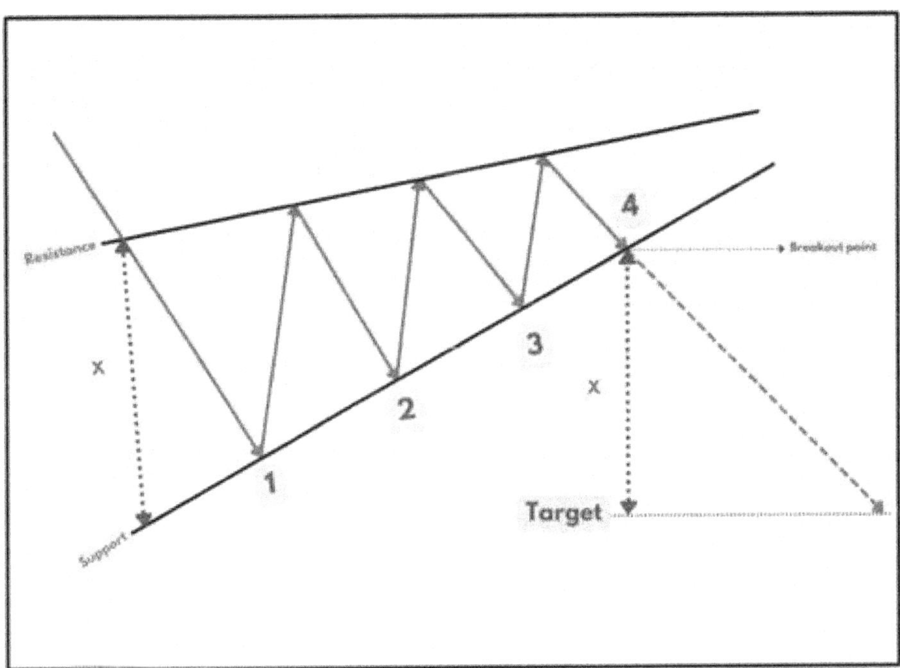

Figure 11.1

A rising wedge pattern looks similar to triangle patterns but works differently. The rising wedge is a bearish chart pattern formed by two rising trendlines. It is a bearish continuation pattern in a downtrend. When a rising wedge forms in an uptrend, it is considered a reversal pattern that changes the price direction to the downside.

Rule of thumb:

1. The price movement inside a Rising wedge Pattern usually breaks at thedownside.

2. Most of the time, the price breaks down from a Rising wedge Pattern onthe 4th or 5th touch on the Support line.

3. When the price breaks downwards, the next target is the height of the Risingwedge Pattern. (If the height of the wedge is 'X' points, then the price will break downwards 'X' points)

Figure 11.2

Figure 11.2 shows the daily chart of the Russel 2000 Index.

Here the price is in an uptrend which moves inside two rising trend lines,forming the Rising Wedge Pattern. The height of the Rising wedge is X points.

The price inside the wedge touched the lower support line four times and brokedown from there on the fifth touch. Then there was a sharp fall in the price towards the next target: X points downfrom the breakout point.

Falling Wedge Pattern

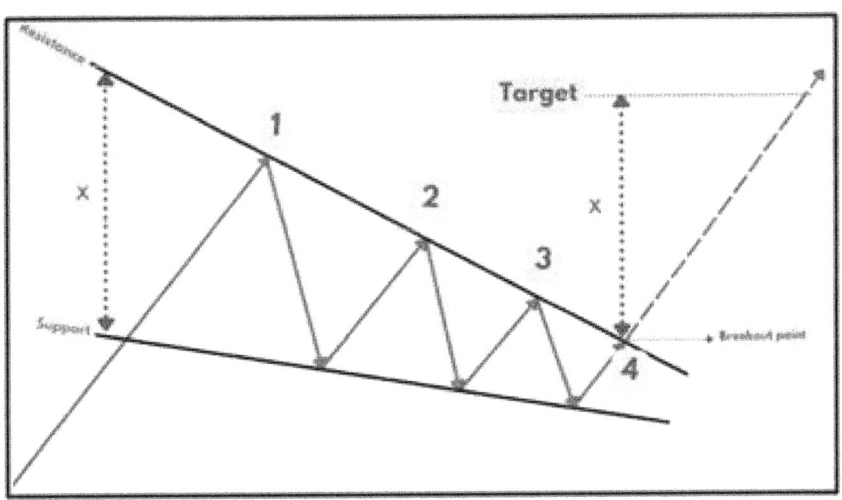

Figure 12.1

A falling wedge pattern is just the opposite of a rising wedge pattern. It is abullish chart pattern formed by two falling trendlines. In an up trend, It is a bullish continuation pattern. When formed in a downtrend, a falling wedge pattern is considered a reversal pattern that changes price direction to the upper side.

Rule of thumb:

1. The price movement inside a falling wedge pattern usually breaks at the upper side when in an up trend.

2. When in a downtrend, the falling wedge Pattern reverses the price direction to the upper side.

3. The price usually breaks out upwards from a falling wedge pattern onthe 4th or 5th touch on the Resistance line.

4. When the price breaks upwards, the next target is the height of the fallingwedge pattern. (If the height of the wedge is 'X' points, then the price will break upward 'X' points).

Figure 12.2

Figure 12.2 shows the daily price chart of Gold Spot/US Dollar.

Here the price is in an uptrend which moves inside two falling trend lines,forming the Falling Wedge Pattern. The height of the Falling wedge is X points.

The price inside the wedge touched three times on the top resistance line andbroke upwards on the fourth touch.

Then there was a sharp increase in the price towards the next target: X pointsupwards from the breakout point.

Head & Shoulder Pattern

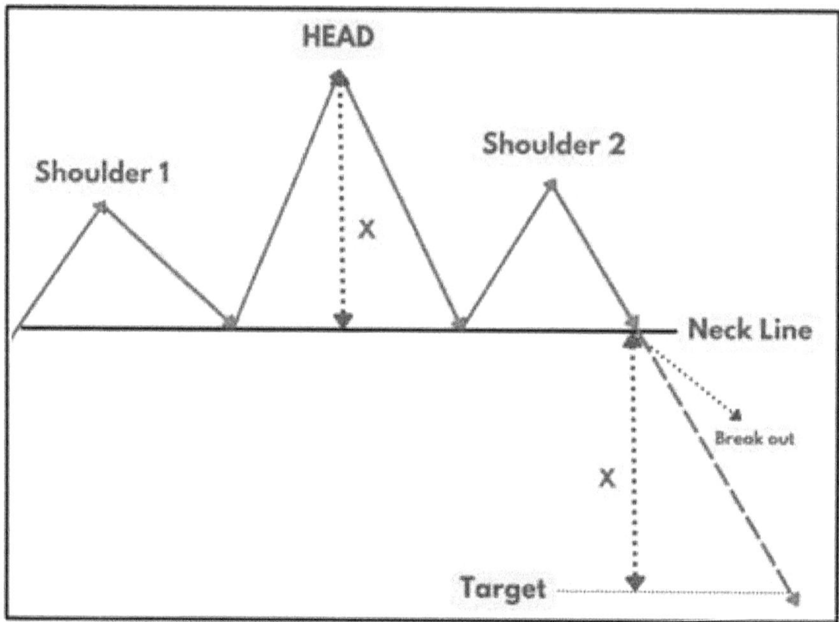

Figure 13.1

Head & shoulder is one of the most analyzed and highly effective patterns to predict the price movement of a financial asset. The Head & Shoulder pattern consists of three peaks. One Head peak and two shoulder peaks on either side of the head peak. There is a shallow trough between the left shoulder and head and another shallow trough between the right shoulder and head. It is a strong reversal patternthat indicates the end of an uptrend. When this pattern is completed, intelligenttraders switch to aggressive selling mode.

Rule of thumb:

1. The Head & shoulder pattern indicates bearish price movement.

2. The price usually breaks at the neckline to the downside.

3. When the price breaks downwards, the next target is the height of the Head (Ifthe height of the head is 'X' points, then the price will break downwards 'X' points)

4. Sometimes, a head and shoulder pattern appears with one extra shoulder,indicating a powerful bearish movement.

Figure 13.2

Figure 13.2 shows the Weekly Forex price chart of the British pound/JapaneseYen.

The upward price movement falls back to the support line (the Neckline) 3 times, forming three peaks. The middle peak, the Head, is bigger than the left and right shoulder peaks. The height of the Head peak is X points.

The price movement in the Head & shoulder pattern breaks down from the Neckline support and goes downwards. The price moves to the target, which is X points downwards.

Inverse Head & Shoulder Pattern

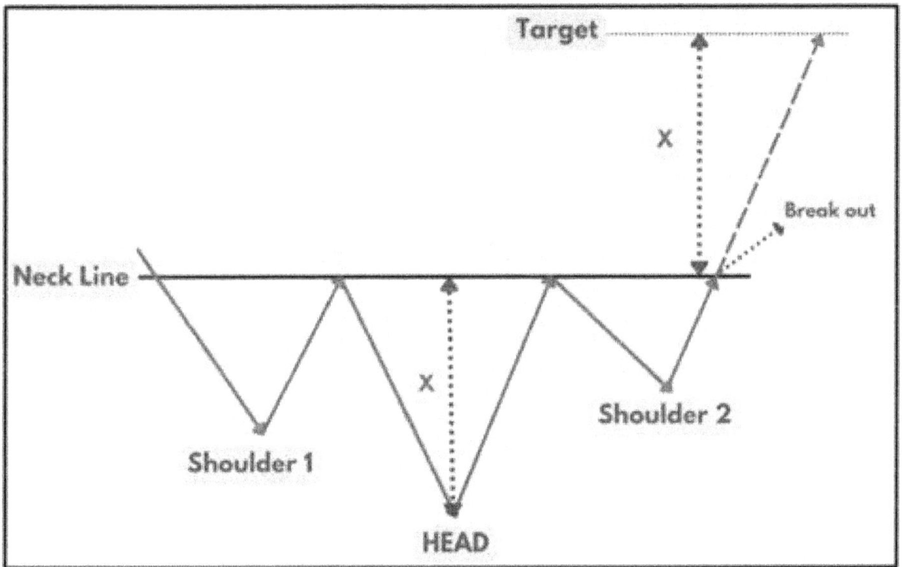

Figure 14.1

The Inverse Head & Shoulder pattern is a strong reversal pattern that results in solid bullish movement. It is just the opposite of the standard Head & shoulderpattern. This pattern mostly appears in a downtrend, which indicates the reversal ofa downtrend to an uptrend. Smart traders start to buy aggressively when the Inverse Head & Shoulder pattern is completed.

Rule of thumb:

1. Inverse Head & Shoulder pattern indicates bullish price movement.

2. The price usually breaks at the neckline to the upper side.

3. When the price breaks upwards, the next target is the height of the invertedHead (If the height of the Head is 'X' points, then the price will break upwards 'X' points)

4. If an inverse head and shoulder pattern appears with one extra shoulder, itindicates a powerful bullish movement.

Figure 14.2

Figure 14.2 shows the daily forex chart of Euro/USD.

The price movement touched the resistance line (the Neckline) 3 times, forming three inverted peaks(One Head & two Shoulders). The height of the Head peak from the Neckline is X points.

The Inverted Head and shoulder price movement breaks up from the Neckline support and goes upwards.

The price moves X points to the target and in the upward direction.

Cup & Handle Pattern

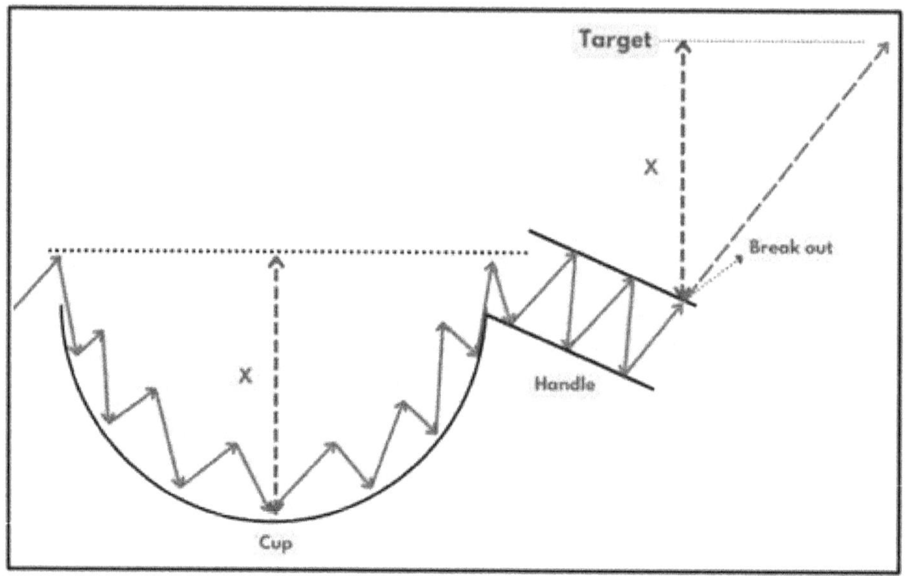

Figure 15.1

The cup & handle pattern is a bullish continuation pattern. The formation of this pattern in an uptrend indicates that the price will continue to move in the upward direction. In this pattern, the price movement forms the shape of a bowl or a cup. Then the price consolidates for a short period in the form of a descending channel or sometimes a flat rectangle, becoming the handle. The price usually breaks upwards from this handle.

Rule of thumb:

1. The cup and handle pattern indicates bullish price movement.

2. The shape of the cup is significant. The cup & handle pattern must have a "U"rather than a "V" shape, with both edges of the cup almost at the same level.

3. The cup handle can be a descending channel or a flat rectangle from where thebreakout happens upwards.

4. The target is the cup's height (If the cup's height is 'X' points, then the pricewill break upward 'X' points).

Figure 15.2

Figure 15.2 shows the Cup & Handle pattern on the Euro/US Dollar Forex price chart.

First, the price moves down and goes back upwards, forming the shape of abowl. The price then consolidates inside a channel for some time, forming the Descending channel and completing the Cup & Handle pattern. The height of theCup is X points.

The price breaks out of the Handle(Descending channel) in the upward direction. There is a sharp increase in price towards the target, which is X points away in the upward direction.

Inverted Cup & Handle Pattern

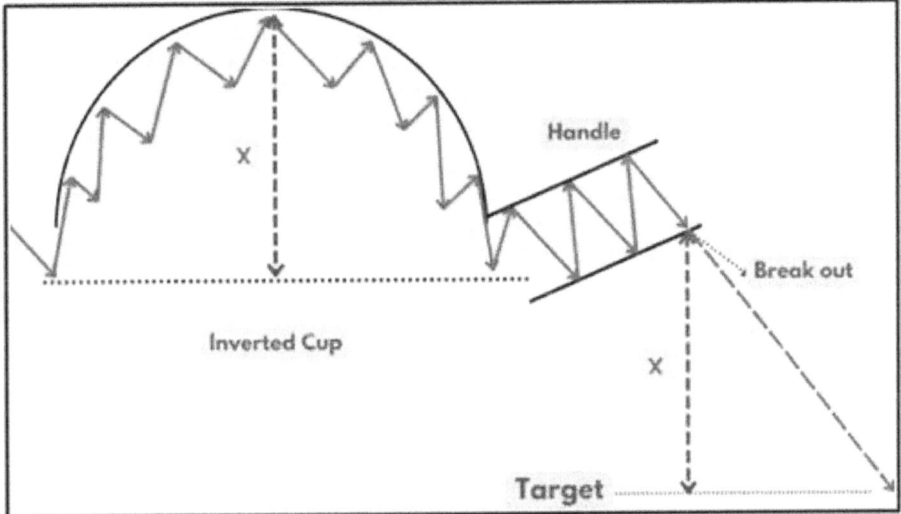

Figure 16.1

The Inverted cup & handle pattern is opposite to the cup & handle pattern. The Inverted cup & handle is a bearish continuation pattern. The price moves in theshape of an inverted semi-circle followed by an ascending channel. This completesthe Inverted Cup & handle pattern. The price usually breaks downwards from the handle.

73

Rule of thumb:

1. The Inverted cup and handle pattern indicates bearish price movement.

2. The shape of the cup is significant. The Cup & handle pattern must have a "U"rather than a "V" shape, with both edges of the cup almost at the same level.

3. The cup handle can be an ascending channel or a flat rectangle, from wherethe breakout happens downwards.

4. The target is the cup's height (If the Cup's height is 'X' points, then the pricewill break downwards 'X' points).

Figure 16.2

Figure 16.2 shows the daily forex price chart of
the Euro/US Dollar. The price moves up and
down, forming an inverted cup shape.
The price moves up inside a small ascending channel and
then breaks out of thechannel downwards.

The price breaks out of the Handle(Ascending channel) in
the downwarddirection.

There is a sharp decrease in price towards the target,
which is X points awayfrom the breakout po

Chapter III
Fibonacci

What are Fibonacci numbers?

How is it useful in trading in financial markets?

Fibonacci numbers were introduced in the west in 1202 by Leonardo Fibonacci. The numbers 0 & 1 are the base Fibonacci numbers.

With 0 and 1 as the first two Fibonacci numbers, the following number in the Fibonacci sequence is derived by adding the last number with the previous number.

Eg: 0, 1, 1, 2, 3, 5, 8, 13, 21, 34, 55, 89, 144...

Now comes the exciting part. Fibonacci numbers come in a natural sequence. The Fibonacci sequence is also found in nature. For example, researchers found that the number of petals of most flowers in the world follows the Fibonacci sequence. Most flowers have petals 5, 8, 13, 21, etc. Even the cones in a pineapple follow the Fibonacci sequence. The breeding cycles of various animals also follow a Fibonacci number. Surprisingly, even the measurements of human body parts follow the Fibonacci sequence.

The total height of any human body divided by the length from our Naval to feet also follows a Fibonacci Golden ratio.

Fibonacci Golden Ratio

Select any Fibonacci number in the sequence to find the Fibonacci Golden ratio.Divide that number by the same number will give the first golden ratio.
Divide the previous Fibonacci number by the chosen number to get the secondGolden ratio, and so on.

The Fibonacci golden ratio is derived by dividing any Fibonacci number by thefollowing number in sequential order.

Eg: 0, 1, 1, 2, 3, 5, 8, 13, 21, 34, 55, 89, 144...

Consider the above Fibonacci numbers.

Let's take number 144 and find the golden ratio.

144/144 = 1

89/144 = 0.618

55/144 = 0.382

34/144 = 0.236

So the above numbers 1, 0.618, 0.382, and 0.236 are called the Fibonacci GoldenRatio.

While used in trading, these numbers are converted to percentage, i.e., 23.6%,38.2%, 61.8% & 100%.

Let us see how to use this fantastic technique in the stock market to predict pricemovements.

1) Fibonacci retracement

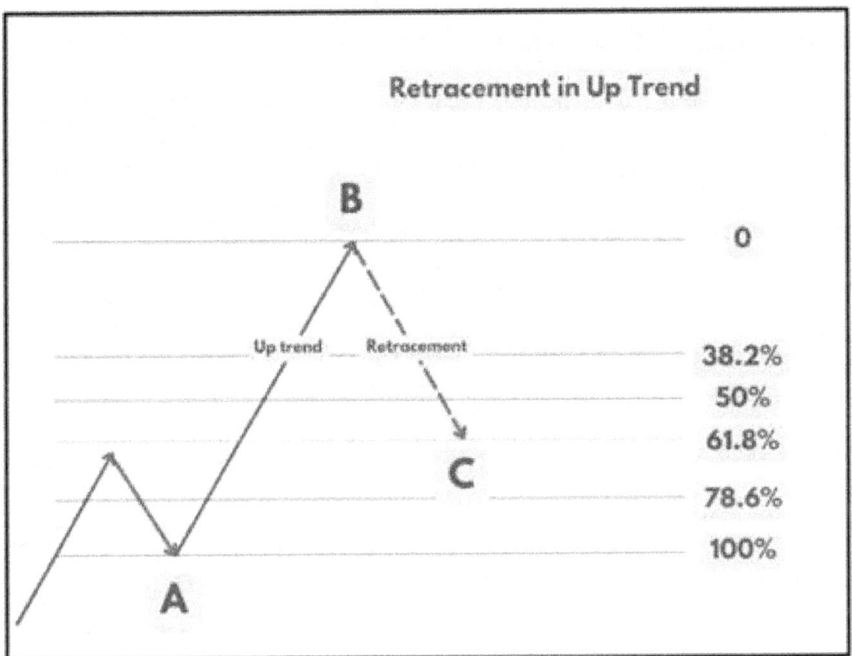

Figure 3.1.1

Traders use the Fibonacci retracement tool to predict/forecast the possible price movement when a powerful upward or downward trend takes a direction change.For example, consider an up trend; the shift in the direction of the uptrend to a downtrend before going up again can be termed a retracement.

When a direction change happens, Plotting Fibonacci retracement will give the traders some idea about the next possible price movement, i.e., 38.2%, 50%, 61.8%, 78.6%, and 100%. Of course, 50% is not a Fibonacci Number, but traders considerthis a crucial level in technical analysis trading. Most of the top traded stocks, currencies, and commodities obey the Fibonacci levels to a great extent.

A Fibonacci retracement forecast is created by taking two extreme points on achart and dividing the vertical distance by important Fibonacci ratios. 0% is the startof the retracement, while 100% is a complete reversal of the original price before the move. Horizontal lines are drawn in the chart for these price levels to providesupport and resistance. Common levels are 23.6%, 38.2%, 50%, 61.8%, 78.6% and
100%.

In the above figure moved the price from point A to point B. The forecast ofprice movement to point C can be created by connecting point A and point B (Swing low to Swing high) using the Fibonacci retracement tool. Then it will show the retracement levels to point C, which will act as the possible future target. Intelligent traders use this highly effective tool to predict price movement and other patterns. Once the retracement begins, they will start selling and riding the profits whileobserving the Fibonacci levels.

Rule of thumb:

1. The majority of ordinary traders use Fibonacci retracement for price forecasts. But most trades hit a stop loss or result in a significant loss.

2. The problem here is that one cannot predict up to which level the retracement will happen(23.6%, 38.2%, 50%, 61.8%, or 78.6%).

3. So, the practical solution to this problem is to do **a Character analysis** of the stock/currency/commodity.

4. Most traders know about the Fibonacci tool but use it the wrong way and lose. On the other hand, intelligent traders understand and use the tool efficiently to bag profits.

Character analysis

Just like humans, the price movement of every stock/currency/commodity hassome characteristic behavior. So, observing the past performance of a financial asset eases the process of understanding its character and, to some extent, helps to predictits future price movement in the market. Therefore, it is necessary to look into that asset's historical charts and analyze how it behaved in the past. Then, using the Fibonacci tools, investors can check past price movements and identify which Fibonacci level the asset follows.

For example: consider a company named XYZ.

By the historical chart analysis, it is found that:

XYZ stock has followed 61.8%
Fibonacci levels 65% of the time

XYZ stock has followed 78.6%
Fibonacci levels 8% of the time

XYZ stock has followed 23.6%
Fibonacci levels 10% of the time

XYZ stock has followed 50%
Fibonacci levels 7% of the time
XYZ stock has followed 38.2%
Fibonacci levels 10% of the time

1. This means that 90% of the time, the XYZ stock is retracing up to 38.2%Fibonacci levels.

2. 80% of the time, the XYZ stock is retracing up to 50% Fibonacci levels.

3. 73% of the time, the XYZ stock is retracing up to 61.8% Fibonacci levels.

Keeping this information in mind, one can use the Fibonacci retracement tool to predict future price movement, increase the probability of winning trades, and trade more confidently. It's effortless. Right?

These are some of the unique secrets the smart traders use to outsmart the other majority of traders. They usually don't share their secrets with anyone. That is whythis is the least discussed topic even on the internet.

Figure 3.1.2

Figure 3.1.2 shows the daily price chart of the Gold spot/US Dollar.

The figure shows the retracement of the price movement from point A to point B.

The price moved upward from point A to point B and retraced to the future price point C.

Using the Fibonacci tool, the first price point A is connected to point B to get theretracement levels.

Here the price touched the critical golden ratio of 61.8% (point C) and bouncedback from that level.

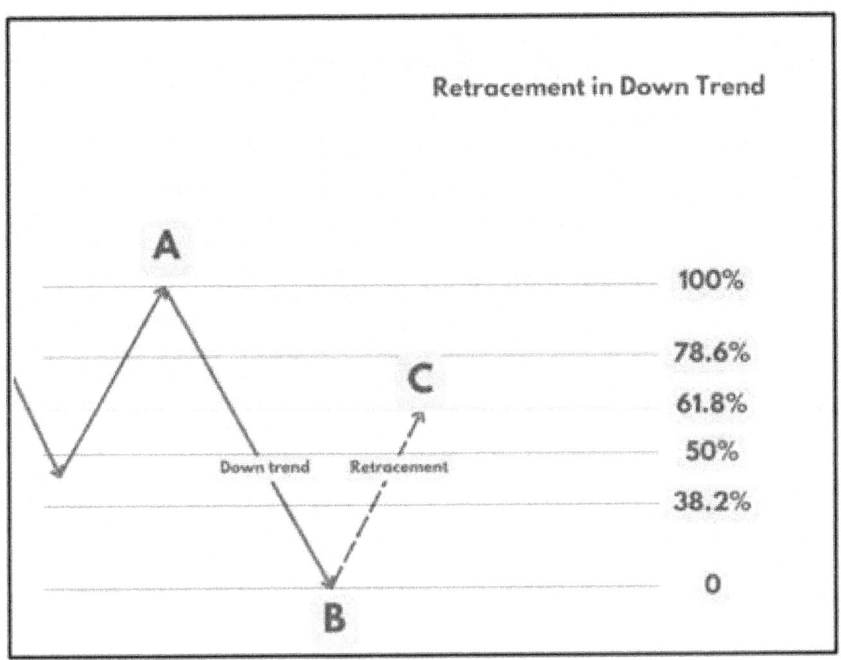

Figure 3.1.3

The above picture shows Fibonacci retracement in the downtrend. Here the price was falling and took a U-turn. In such a scenario, use the tool to create Fibonacci retracement from point A to Point B (Swing high to swing low). Then it will plotthe possible Fibonacci retracement levels to which the price may increase. Once the retracement begins, traders usually go to buy the asset.

Figure 3.1.4

Figure 3.1.4 shows the daily price chart of the Gold spot/US Dollar.

The figure shows the Fibonacci retracement for price movement in a downward direction. Here the price moved downwards from point A to point B and took a U-turn to retrace to point C.

By connecting points A and B using the Fibonacci tool, the retracement of priceto the future price point C is determined. The chart clearly shows that the price retracement touched the Fibonacci levels of 61.8% and

71.6% (point C), respectively.

2) Fibonacci Extension

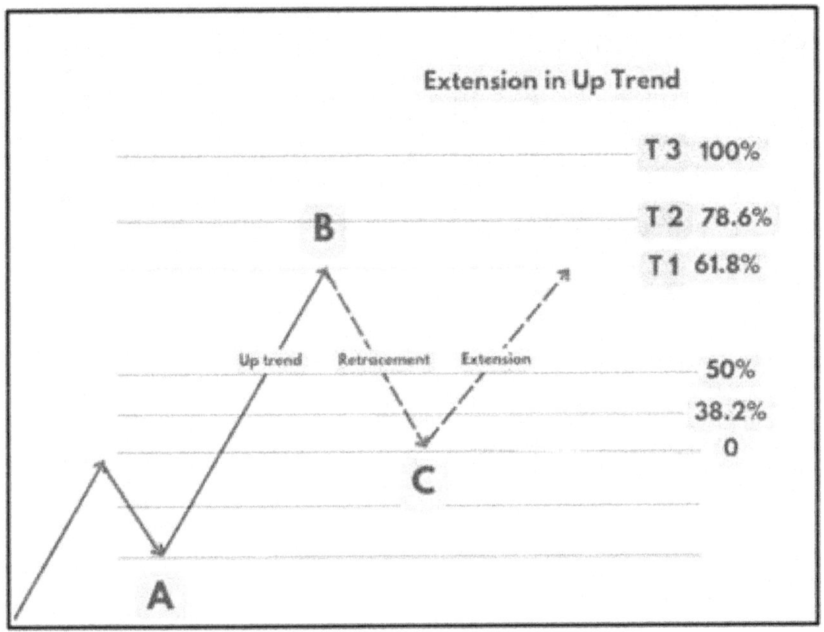

Figure 3.2.1

A Fibonacci extension is an effective tool traders use to determine potential profit targets or estimate how far a price may go after a pullback. There is also a possibility that the price will reverse at extension levels. Like Fibonacci retracement, the Fibonacci extension levels are also based on Fibonacci ratios (as percentages). Common Fibonacci extension levels are 61.8%, 78.6%, 100%, 161.8%, 200% etc.

The above figure shows the movement of the price from point A to point B(swing low to swing high). Then, it is retraced back to point C. Plotting these 3 points using the Fibonacci extension tool will show the following levels to whichthe price would move(61.8%, 100%, 161.8% ...etc.).

Figure 3.2.2

Figure 3.2.2 shows the daily price chart of the Us Dollar/Swiss Franc.

Here, consider the upward price movement from point A to point B, which thenretraces to point C.

Plot the Fibonacci Extension tool on the price chart, Starting from point A topoint B & then to point C to get possible future targets T1, T2, T3 & T4.

The chart clearly shows the price movement hitting the target levels T1, T2, T3& T4 upward.

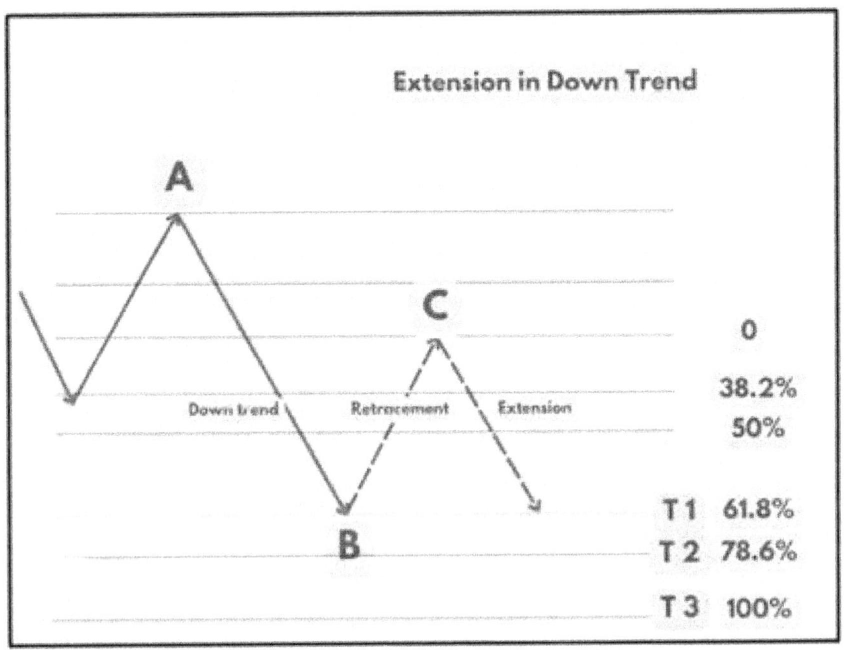

Figure 3.2.3

Connect points A(high) to B(low) and then C(retracement) using the Fibonacci extension tool. This tool will plot the possible target levels and give the trader anidea of up to which levels the price will move next.

How Fibonacci extension differs from fibonacci retracement?

Fibonacci retracements measure the pullbacks within a trend. In contrast, Fibonacci extensions measure the impulse waves within the trend direction. Fibonacci retracement levels indicate how deep a retracement might be. At the same time, extensions show where the price will go following a retracement.

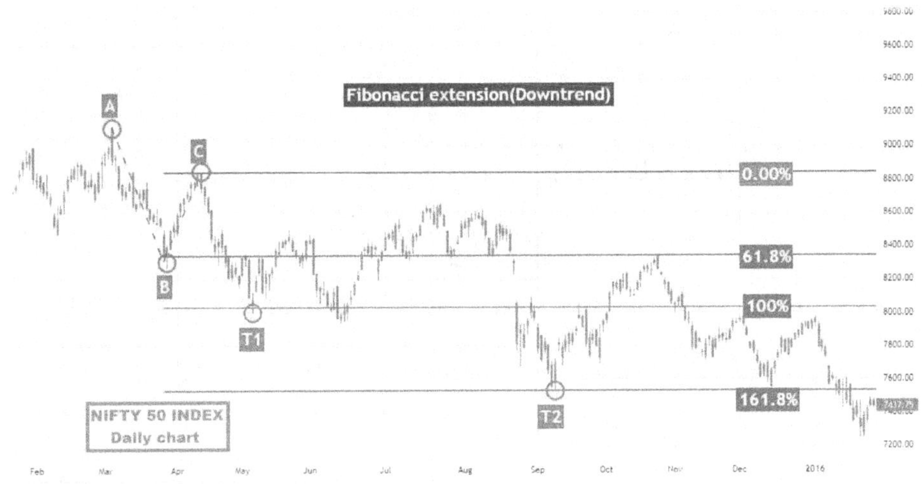

Figure 3.2.4

Figure 3.2.4 shows the daily chart of Nifty 50, NSE.

Here consider the downward price movement from point A to point B, whichthen retraced to point C.

Following the steps previously used in Figure 3.2.3, plot the Fibonacci Extension tool on the price chart, starting from point A to point B & then to point C. The Fibonacci Extension tool will show the possible future targets T1 & T2.

The chart clearly shows the price movement hitting the target levels T1 & T2 inthe downward direction.

Chapter IV
<u>Indicators</u>

In technical analysis, a technical indicator is a calculator that uses historic price, volume, and open interest information to predict the direction of a financial market. The market constantly switches between bullish and bearish modes. Moreover, the strength and duration of the trend(uptrend and downtrend) also change with time.Here technical indicators can be of great help.

There are four types of Technical indicators: Trend indicators, Momentum indicators, Volume indicators, and Volatility indicators.

Here we will discuss Trend and Momentum indicators.

Trend indicators:

Trend indicators measure trend direction. These indicators also help to find outthe strength of a particular trend. One of the most used trend indicators is the Moving average indicator.

Moving average (MA)

A moving average is an indicator of a trend calculated by averaging the closing prices of past trading sessions over time. The moving average creates a constantly updated average price line which smoothes out price data on time. As a result of creating a single, flat line on a price chart, a moving average eliminates any effectsof random price fluctuations. Traders take an average of several periods, such as ten days, 20 minutes, 30 weeks, or any period they choose. Among the most popular simple moving averages for investors and trend followers are the 200-day, 100-day, and 50-day moving averages. The angle of movement of moving averages shows whether the price movement is trending or ranging. The horizontal direction of the moving average shows that the price is ranging or in consolidation. If the Moving average is moving upward, it shows an up trend. But it doesn't mean that the pricewill go up. Instead, it shows an overall picture of the trend direction depending onthe previous price movements.

Trade Setup using Moving Average

Plot the two moving averages, 50 days and 200 days, on the same price chart.

When the two moving averages cross each other, it indicates an opportunity tobuy or sell.

A Buy signal is formed when the 50-day moving average exceeds the 200-day moving average.

A Sell signal is formed when the 200-day moving average exceeds the 50-day moving average.

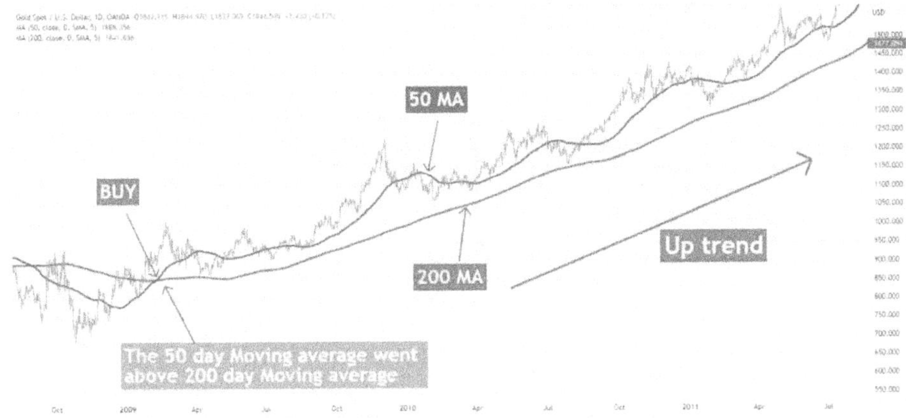

Figure 4.1.1

Figure 4.1.1 shows the daily chart of Gold Spot/US Dollar.

Here 50-Day Moving Averages & 200-Day Moving averages are plotted on the price chart. The blue line shows the 50-Day MA, and the Red line shows the 200-Day MA.

When the price changed from the Lowest point to Higher High(HH), the 50-day Moving Average exceeded the 200 Day Moving Average. This indicates Price movement in the upward direction.

As seen in the figure, the price continued to move in the uptrend for some time, with 50 Day MA still above 200 Day MA.

Figure 4.1.2

Figure 4.1.2 shows the daily chart of Gold Spot/US Dollar.

As in Figure 4.1, the 50-Day Moving Averages & 200-Day Moving averages are plotted on the price chart. When the price changed from the Highest point to Lower High(LH), the 50-day Moving Average crossed below the 200 Day Moving Average. This indicates price movement in the downward direction.

The chart/info graph indicates that the price continued to move in the Downtrend for some time, with the 50-Day MA line below the 200-Day MA line.

Momentum indicators

The momentum indicators are technical analysis tools that determine how reasonable or weak a stock's price is. The momentum indicators measure the rate at which stock prices rise or fall. One of the most commonly used momentum indicators is the Relative Strength Index.

Relative Strength Index (RSI)

The relative strength index (RSI) is a technical indicator that measures the speed and fluctuations of the price. J. Welles Wilder developed it in 1978. When plottedon a price chart, RSI assigns stocks a value between 0 and 100. The RSI levels oscillate between values zero and 100. The RSI indicator has two warning levels to indicate overselling and overbuying. Levels 70 and 30 are standard levels that serveas a warning system for overbought and oversold assets.

Trade Setup using RSI

Plot a 14-day RSI on any price chart. [RSI(14)]

When RSI is above 70, the stock is considered overbought, so the price couldstart falling.

When RSI is below 30, the stock price is considered oversold; this paves the way for a bullish price movement anytime.

For better results, use 14-Day RSI along with the 50-Day Moving average and 200-Day Moving average.

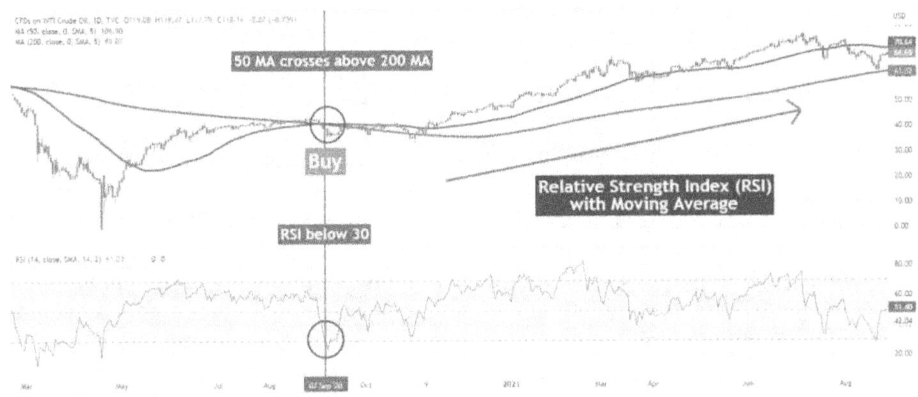

Figure 4.2.1

Figure 4.2.1 shows the daily price chart of WTI Crude oil.

Here the indicator's 14-day RSI, 50-Day Moving Average, and 200-Day Moving Average are plotted on the price chart. In the beginning, RSI was lower, but the 50- Day Moving average was below the 200-Day Moving Average.

The figure shows that the 50-day Moving Average exceeds the 200 Day Moving Average. At the same time, RSI was at 27 levels. This indicates strong price movement in the upward direction. The price continued to move in the uptrend for some more time, with 50 Day MA still above 200 Day MA.

How effective is pattern trading?

People always have a question in mind about the effectiveness of pattern trading. For example, some may wonder how often a pattern appears in a chart or does it take longer time durations for a pattern to complete so that they can enter a trade.

The exciting thing is that some pattern formation exists in different time framesif you take any price chart.

For example, if you take the price chart of XYZ company, you could find apattern formed in the monthly time frame. When you switch to the weekly timeframe of the same chart, you will find another pattern. The same happens with daily 4 hours, 1 hours, 15 minutes, and 5 minutes charts of the same company.

There also exist possibilities of multiple pattern formations in the same timeframe of the price chart.

Figure 4.2.2

Figure 4.2.2 shows the forex daily price chart of the USD/INR. The data illustrates multiple patterns formed in the daily timeframe of the USD/INR pricechart. First, a Symmetric Triangle is formed, followed by one Ascending channel andtwo Descending channels. All four price patterns hit the Target level per the pattern trading rules.

The trades carried out on four pattern formations (three buy and one sell indication) gave excellent returns. If analyzed further, one can identify more patterns in the same chart and with different time frames.

Chapter V
<u>Trade Discipline</u>

There was a professional trainer who trained hundreds of people in trading in thefinancial markets.

He had a set of new traders who were getting started in trading.

The trainer taught them all the basics, how to do fundamental and technicalanalysis, and all the new tools needed for trading.

He demonstrates specific trading strategies and tells them what they should andshouldn't do.

But unfortunately, this trainer couldn't seem to get his traders to make money.The traders tried everything they could but still lost money in the markets.
The trainer was also frustrated because of the trader's failures.

So one day, he got an idea and devised a strategy to assist his traders inbecoming more profitable.

He invented a ground-breaking new method of training them.He instructed them to make three trades.

And they have to do something wild with these three trades.

Instead of seeking ways to make money, they must lose money on all three tradings in a row.

That means they'll have to lose money on trade 1, trade 2, and trade 3.

The idea seemed simple, but the traders couldn't even get it right this time! Themajority of those trades ended up in **profits**!!!

So here is the moral of the story.

You should consider changing your trading strategy if you're doing everythingright and it isn't making you money in the long run.

We have now learned about various trading methods using Patterns, Fibonacci,and Indicators. We have now arrived at the most critical chapter of this book, whichis:

"Trade discipline."

Now here comes the exciting part:

What if I told you that you could make money from trading without usingtools or strategies?

Yes. It is possible!

The secret lies in **Trade Discipline**.

Whatever the market condition, you can make money quickly by having a TradeDiscipline, which is more important than any tools or strategies.

To have a Trade discipline, you need
to follow two things.They are:

1. Position sizing

2. Risk Reward ratio

Position sizing

90% of traders fail because of not having any Trade discipline. These tradersknow how to trade, but they do not know how much quantity of shares or commodities to buy or sell per trade. Instead, they trade with all their capital in their trading account, which is not the right thing to do. In addition, they do not know anything about Position Sizing.

The position sizing strategy has only one thumb rule:

"Do not risk more than 1% of your capital in any single trade".

How much quantity to buy or sell in a particular trade is determined by three factors:

The capital you have for trading

The risk per share/commodity you are willing to take

(Share price – Stop Loss) Cost of the Stock or commodity

For Example, You have a capital of 100,000$ in your Trading Account.

Capital in Trading account	100,000
1% of Capital (Maximum risk per trade)	1000
The stock price	100
Stop Loss	95
Maximum risk per share	5

The ideal trading quantity = Maximum Risk you take in a trade / Maximum risk per share = 1000/5 = 200 shares.

In this trade setup, if anything goes wrong and your stop-loss hits, all you canlose is 1% of your capital, which is 1000$.

Here you have the capital to enter 100 different trades, meaning you must bewrong in 100 trades to lose all your money in your trading account. I am sure that that's very unlikely.

For a successful trade setup, traders must use a position sizing strategy anda Risk Reward Ratio.

In the above example,

Suppose you use the position sizing strategy correctly and a Risk reward ratio of 1:3. In that case, even if you lose 70 trades out of 100 trades, you will still be in profit with just 30 winning trades.

To understand it better, let's learn about the Risk Reward Ratio.

Risk Reward Ratio

The risk-reward ratio is a measure of return in terms of risk for a specific period.

Using this ratio, you can estimate the expected return per unit of risk on a trade.

Investors and traders follow the risk-reward ratio to protect their capital amount. Trades and investors with excellent trade discipline follow the Risk-Reward ratio to generate consistent profits. There are different Risk Reward ratios for a trader to choose from. The most commonly used ratios are 1:1.5, 1:2, and 1:3. Successful traders do the following while using Risk reward Ratio:

1. Choose the risk and reward level according to their strategy.

2. A risk-to-reward ratio of over 1.0 indicates greater potential risk than a potential reward; anything below 1.0 suggests that the potential profit is greater than the potential risk.

3. The more the reward, the longer becomes the trade duration.

4. No matter what happens in trades, never square off positions before reaching profit or loss positions defined by the selected Risk Reward Ratio.

Risk Reward (1 : 1.5)

Win	Profit/trade	Total	Loss	Loss/Trade	Total	Net Profit/Loss
6	1500	9000	4	-1000	-4000	5000
4	1500	6000	6	-1000	-6000	0
3	1500	4500	7	-1000	-7000	-2500

Risk = 1000   Reward = 1500   Total Trades = 10

Here the trader decides to take the risk of 1 for a return of 1.5.Risk = 1000 for a reward of 1500.

Let us see what happens if the trader wins four trades and loses six trades.Win : 4 x 1500 = 6000

Loss : 6 x 1000 = 6000

Gain – Loss = **0**

In this setup, even if the trader loses six out of 10 trades and succeeds only in 4of the trades, the **net profit/ loss** is **Zero**.

With this risk-reward ratio, your capital is safe even if you lose **60%** of yourtotal trades.

Risk Reward (1 : 2)

Win	Profit/trade	Total	Loss	Loss/Trade	Total	Net Profit/Loss
6	2000	12000	4	-1000	-4000	8000
4	2000	8000	6	-1000	-6000	2000
3	2000	6000	7	-1000	-7000	-1000

Risk = 1000   Reward = 2000   Total Trades = 10

Here the trader decides to take the risk of 1 for a return of 2.
Risk = 1000 for reward of 2000.

Let us see what happens if the trader wins three trades and loses seven trades. Win : 3 x 2000 = 6000

Loss : 7 x 1000 = 7000

Gain – Loss = **-1000**

In this setup, even if the trader loses seven out of ten trades and succeeds only in Three trades, the **net loss** is the risk amount, i.e., **1000**.

This means that with this risk-reward ratio, even if you lose 60% of your total trades, you can still end up at a profit. If you lose 70% of your total tradings, your losses will be marginal.

Risk Reward (1 : 3)

Win	Profit/trade	Total	Loss	Loss/Trade	Total	Net Profit/Loss
6	3000	18000	4	-1000	-4000	14000
4	3000	12000	6	-1000	-6000	6000
3	3000	9000	7	-1000	-7000	2000

Risk = 1000   Reward = 3000   Total Trades = 10

Here the trader decides to take the risk of 1 for a return of 2. Risk = 1000 for a reward of 2000.

> Let us see what happens if the trader wins three trades and loses seven trades.Win : 3 x 3000 = 9000
>
> Loss : 7 x 1000 = 7000
>
> Gain – Loss   = **+2000**

In this setup, even if the trader loses seven out of 10 trades and succeeds only inThree trades, the **net profit** is **2000**.

This means that with this risk-reward ratio, even if you lose 70% of your totaltrades, you can still end up at a profit.

Heads or tails?

Are you ready to play a game to test the success rate of the Risk-Reward Ratio?If the answer is YES!!, then read the following:

(**Disclaimer**: Here, the writer suggests making artificial trades strictly for educational purposes to test the success rate of the Risk Reward ratio. NOT onactual trades with real money.)

Things you will need:

1. A mock/dummy/artificial trading account (if you don't have one, do papertrading, that is, you make imaginary trades with the real-time price of Stock/ currency/ commodities)

2. A coin

3. A book and a pencil

The steps are as follows:

1. Select a Risk-Reward Ratio (1:2 or 1:3 etc.)

2. Flip the coin.

3.If you get heads, go for an immediate BUY in the
   dummy trading account.

4. If you get tails, go for a SELL.

5. Make at least ten trades (the more the number of trades, the better) with strictstop loss and target set according to the selected Risk-Reward ratio.

6. Evaluate the results and calculate the overall profit/loss.

The results will be surprising.

Even if 60% of executed trades result in losses, overall trades result in profits.

This experiment means one does not need all the knowledge to become a successful trader. He requires a good Risk-Reward Ratio, trade discipline, and just a coin to succeed in trading. In addition to that, the winning chances and profits oftrades improve with using technical analysis such as pattern trading/ Fibonacci/ indicators.

Now here is the frequently asked question:

If this strategy that successful, what is the need for technical analysis?

Answer: There are three conditions in a financial market, Upward movement, downward movement and sideways movement. This strategy works well when the market is in an active state, when there is a strong upward or downward movement, resulting in better profits. But suppose the market goes sideways, almost like adormant state. In that case, the profits will be lesser as the price may not move up to the targets as per the calculated risk-reward ratio. In that case, one can use technical analysis to determine whether a sudden movement is expected in the market.

How to Win at the Stock Market: mental muscle-building books to sharpen your mind

The stock market is an arena of warriors. The only way to survive there, if you want to play long-term, is to be mentally prepared for any situation that might come up. The world of finance can be unpredictable, so you need to be ready to face whatever comes your way to win the game. You need to build mental muscles and sharpen your mind to do this. The good news is that books are a great tool that can help you achieve this goal.

Books to Sharpen Your Mind

Reading can improve your memory. By reading, you improve your ability to remember things. The more you read, the better your brain will retain informationand recall it accurately in various situations.

Trading in financial markets is truly a mind game. Only sharp and strong-minded traders can survive longer with consistent profits. One can master this skill through constant learning

and practice.

Conclusion

It is a universal truth that everything in this world, including our life, circumstances, situations, and even our future, is uncertain. One cannot predict what will or will not happen next, and the stock market works the same. It is impossible to expect precisely which way the price will go. Sometimes, even when all thepatterns and indicators clearly show a direction of the market, it goes the oppositeway. Situations like war, pandemics, disasters, Government policies, a conflict between countries, etc., could scare investors and create chaos in the market.

These rare situations do not occur every time. But it could cause enormous lossesto ordinary traders and investors. On the other hand, many traders with good trade discipline and money management skills profit significantly from these uncertain situations. Every trader in the market, whether a small or a prominent institutional trader, is susceptible to these situations. No one has control of the financial market. This is because the financial market, a wonderful creation by human beings, operates on two human emotions:

Fear and Desire.

All humans have a fear of losing everything and a desire/greed to gain everything.
Both, in the extreme, are destructive emotions.

We can succeed in the long run if we accept these facts and move ahead with conscious decisions and **trade discipline**.

The information contained in this book is strictly for educational purposes. Therefore, if you wish to apply the ideas in this book, you take full responsibility for your actions.